Creative Space

Creative Space

21 strategies to help calm your chattering mind, clear your busy calendar and create the physical space you need to get your best work done.

by Dominique Falla

First published by Creative Spark 2020

PO Box 27
New Brighton
NSW 2483
Australia

www.creativesparkpodcast.com

For my darling husband George
who gives me all the creative space I need.

Contents

Foreword

The Free Creative Space Companion Course

To help guide you through the Creative Space activities, I have created a free companion course. The course includes downloadable worksheets, videos, and bonus resources.

The free course is designed to help you successfully apply the 21 strategies from this book.

The materials in the free course are organised to match the sections and chapters of the book, making it easy for you watch each video as you read along and complete the activities.

Access the free Creative Space bonus course here:
creativespace.link/course

Preface

About the Book

Creative Space is a practical pocket guide for busy people who desperately want to carve more space for creativity into their lives.

The book is divided into three sections dedicated to helping you find more: headspace, calendar space, and physical space for creativity.

Dominique Falla has written 21 bite-sized chapters with practical activities to help you:

»   Calm your mind, quiet your thoughts, and clear your headspace.
»   Steal time, prioritise effectively, and clear space in your busy calendar.
»   Clear out the clutter, create a dedicated studio, and make space in your life for creativity.

By the time you have finished reading Creative Space, you will have 21 strategies for living a more spacious and creative life.

As a bonus, readers will also gain access to the free companion course, with practical worksheets and videos to help you put ideas into action.

Introduction

Creativity is not only useful for artists, writers, and musicians. Creativity is an essential skill when it comes to problem-solving and resourcefulness in everyday life. You don't have to be an "artist" to benefit from increased levels of creativity—just like you don't need to be an athlete to benefit from increased levels of physical fitness—but who knows what might be unlocked if you start exercising your creative muscles?

Enhanced creativity not only helps with daily problem-solving, but it can also change our perspective on the issues we face. By identifying and clearing creative blocks and living from a place of curiosity instead of fear, we can improve the quality of our lives immeasurably. As a result, creative people are OK with making mistakes and learning from them, rather than avoiding them.

Artists benefit from the creative process of course, but so can the rest of us.

> *"Creativity is just connecting things. When you ask creative people how they did something, they feel a little guilty because they didn't do it, they just saw something. It seemed obvious to them after a while. That's because they were able to connect experiences they've had and synthesise new things"—Steve Jobs*

The ability to make connections between seemingly unrelated concepts, to put situations in a new perspective, to problem-solve in ways that aren't immediately obvious, to create something out of nothing, these are all facets of a creative mind.

For some people, the creative process leads them on to create art or music or poetry or design, but for the majority, creativity can manifest itself in all areas of our daily lives.

The most creative people don't necessarily have to "make" anything; they are living creative lives full of curiosity and making exciting connections.

> *"To be creative means to be in love with life. You can be creative only if you love life enough that you want to enhance its beauty, you want to bring a little more music to it, a little more poetry to it, a little more dance to it"—Osho*

You can look at creativity from an intensely pragmatic viewpoint like Steve Jobs, or take a spiritual approach like Osho. For some, creativity is a way to make a living or to solve everyday problems using lateral thinking; for others, it is their spark, their life force, their reason for being.

Once you start exploring the topic of creativity, you realise it means many things to many people. Still, one thing I do know to be true is that to stand outside the realm of art and think creativity is something that artistic people are "gifted" with is a mistake. Just as wonder and play are universal to all young children, creativity is a common trait in all humanity; it is just that some of us make better use of it than others.

So if we are born with an innate ability to be creative, where does it go? Why does it disappear in some and not in others? Sir Ken Robinson would argue, and many agree with him, that the structured education system polishes it out of us.

If the creative process relies on us being willing to make mistakes, and the education system requires us always to be right, then those two philosophies are fundamentally at odds. For some people, they just don't fit into the traditional education system and their ability to be creative remains intact. For the majority, their schooling and upbringing push all creative urges away, and they "forget" how to be creative. A rare few can tell the difference and do well in the traditional education systems as well as retaining their creativity.

The good news is that creativity is like a muscle. If we don't exercise them, our creativity muscles will simply atrophy. They don't go anywhere, they are still there, waiting for you to use them again. To get the most benefit out of your creative muscles, you need to exercise them regularly.

Maintaining a regular creativity routine will have lasting benefits for your mental health and well-being, just like a physical fitness routine does.

Creative Blocks

People struggle to be creative for a variety of reasons. It might be that your day job or family saps all of your energy, you don't have space or resources, or maybe you think creativity is a frivolous waste of time.

After completing the exercises in this book, you will discover that no matter how busy, restricted, or "uncreative" you are, there are ways to steal time, set priorities, and clear the space you need to be creative. You will soon come to realise that your obstacles are all just "creative blocks", and we will set about clearing them.

As a child, we were all "creative." We painted and drew and told stories and played games for hours every day. We didn't need to be told or shown how to do it, and we didn't need expensive toys, or permission, we just played.

As people grow older, there are fewer opportunities to play. We prioritise school, work, family responsibilities, and the pressures of daily life instead. We didn't become any less creative; we merely allowed our creativity to atrophy. The good news is, your creativity muscles didn't go anywhere; they are quietly waiting for you to exercise them again.

"Creativity is like a muscle. You need to exercise it every day"
—Dominique Falla

This book is divided into three sections: headspace, calendar space, and physical space. They are presented in this particular order because from many years of working with blocked creatives; I find the blocks always appear in this order. Clearing your mind for creativity allows you to carve space on your calendar for creativity and finally claim your own physical space for creativity.

Before you dive in, I have a little gift for you. I have developed a free companion course where I take you through each activity, step by step. I want you to take action and get the most out of these strategies. There are also free downloadable worksheets for some of the exercises.

In just 15-minutes a day, you will learn 21 practical, actionable strategies to help you clear the mental, physical, and calendar space you need to get your most important creative work done.

Are you ready? Let's get started.

Access the free Creative Space bonus course here: creativespace.link/course

1

CREATIVE HEADSPACE

In this section, you will learn how daily journaling will calm your brain chatter and clear space in your mind for creativity. You will discover how to give yourself permission to be creative and say goodbye to those negative voices in your head. You will learn to prioritise your creativity and forgive yourself when you make mistakes. You will uncover the magic of fresh starts and banish energy vampires from your life forever.

Journaling for Mental Clarity

*"Journal to awaken your mind
and transform your life"—Asad Meah*

Brain chatter is a creativity killer

One of the most significant areas where creatives struggle to find space might surprise you. It is not space in your calendar. It is not studio space. Believe it or not, it is space in your brain.

Unless you are a meditation guru and can empty your mind at will, you are probably like most busy people and suffer from brain chatter. You might also know it as the monkey mind, or your inner dialogue, but whatever you call it, it can overwhelm your creative brain.

It is estimated we think between 2000–3000 thoughts per hour, but when you think too many jumbled thoughts or the same ideas over and over again, it makes it difficult to think clearly or creatively.

Thinking too many thoughts all at once can often mean events are moving quickly and you are struggling to keep up with everything that is happening, or it might mean that you are thinking too many steps ahead and not remaining in the present.

Depression often manifests itself as overthinking about the past, and anxiety stems from overthinking about the future.

Obsessing over the same thoughts can also be problematic. You might feel like a broken record going round and round thinking about the same problem. It is easy to get stuck here and not move forward.

Without a clear head and space to think, it is impossible to get your best work done.

Daily journaling is the solution

Meditation is often cited as the solution to calm a busy mind. Still, for many active creatives suffering from brain chatter, deep meditation is challenging to master and usually takes more time than we have available.

Luckily, there is another way to calm your monkey mind—daily journaling.

You might have heard of stream-of-consciousness writing, free-writing, morning pages, brain dumping, and so on. All of these are forms of journaling, designed to clear the mind.

I learned this technique many years ago from Julia Cameron when she wrote about a tool she called Morning Pages in her book *The Artist's Way*.

Julia advocates for writing three A4 pages every morning, which is quite a lot for a beginner like I was. I stuck with the technique, however, and now, I regularly empty my brain into three journal pages as I drink my morning coffee.

I try and journal as often as possible, and I am usually successful five mornings out of every seven. I have used this technique now for the last 21 years, and I credit it with every creative idea I have had since.

Free-writing in a journal might feel strange at first. At school, we learned that our writing must be grammatically correct, and we obsess over punctuation, phrasing, and spelling. For this process to work, however, you have to let go of all those pre-conditioned writing rules. For many people, that takes some practice.

Speed must replace correctness when you do this activity.

To empty your mind onto paper, you must do so without thinking. The way to write without thought is to write fast and continuously, without lifting the pen.

The magic of this process is that once you have cleared enough space in your conscious mind, you make space for your sub-conscious mind to appear on the page.

If you use this technique every morning, you will eventually clear out the clutter, and then it only takes a few minutes to sweep away the brain junk from the last 24 hours.

Stick with the process for a few weeks. The results can be magical.

The primary purpose of free-writing is to empty your mind onto the paper. That means writing down anything and everything that is currently bothering you, or occupying your mind. Write down all the thoughts that are rattling around in your brain. Record all of the mental chatter in all its crazy rambling forms.

An important thing to note at this stage is that you will begin to fill notebooks with what looks like the ramblings of a crazy person.

I try, where possible, to keep all of my journals hidden from prying eyes. If I think that someone is going to read my writing, I begin to censor myself, which is why I make sure to write somewhere private and keep what I have written hidden.

I often write my morning pages in a coffee shop on the way to work. I already had the coffee habit, so it was straightforward to add the journal habit once I made the connection that the two were compatible activities.

If you can't commit to free-writing every day, try it for 15-minutes today and see if your thoughts are calmer afterwards. Keep the tool in your back pocket for those days when your brain chatter gets too loud, or you find yourself thinking the same thoughts over again.

Your goal is to write as many words as possible in 15-minutes, which means letting go of grammar, punctuation or even legibility. When I am in my flow, my writing becomes illegible, and that's OK. Just focus on emptying the words from your head.

It helps to think of the blank page as an empty trash can. When you throw things away, you don't go rummaging through the bin afterwards. The important thing is that you are clearing the words out of your head to make space for creativity. Don't worry about what the words say.

15-minute daily activity

Find a paper journal or a large notepad and choose a pen you like.

I always use a particular brand of ballpoint pen because the ink flow is very smooth and can keep up with the speed of my writing. I also like using spiral-bound artist sketchbooks rather than lined notepaper because I find lines very restrictive when I am writing quickly.

Once you have your pen and notebook, find a quiet place away from distractions, or prying eyes.

Set a timer on your phone for 15-minutes and then put pen to paper.

Don't stop until the timer rings. Don't lift your pen to "think."

Don't check your phone or talk to anyone. Just write solidly for 15-minutes. Don't read what you have written afterwards.

Ready? Set. Start writing!

Give Yourself Permission

"Permission calls us home to ourselves"—Shelby Forsythia

Waiting for someone to grant permission keeps you stuck

Most of us spent the first 18 years of our lives, asking our parents permission to do things, especially if they were fun. Can I go over to Rebecca's house? Can I go to the movies with my friends? Can I get a dog? And so on.

The request was usually met with a firm no. Or a series of questions and negotiations before a yes, but with conditions. Yes, but make sure you are home by nine. Yes, but make sure a parent drives you.

Is it any wonder that when we turned 18 and could do anything we wanted (within reason), we still behaved ourselves because the permission programming was ingrained?

Technically, one of the jobs of a parent is to program good habits that will last us a lifetime. Every time I brush my teeth or wash my hands as an adult, I know it is because of the ingrained programming I received as a child. Every time I go to cross the road,

I look right and left. This childhood programming has saved my life more than once.

However, permission programming is not as useful when we become adults. The idea that we need to ask permission to do something fun no longer serves us, especially if our parents are no longer around. Who do we ask then?

I have a friend who still resists doing silly things because her mother wouldn't approve. Her mother has been dead for 27 years!

Give yourself permission instead

Creativity and taking risks are two of those things which are fun and slightly dangerous. As a teenager, I would have had to ask permission to paint a mural or start a business. How about playing a music gig or going on a creative retreat? You bet.

As an adult, considering any of these creative activities can bring up those same feelings of excitement and dread. We often defer the permission–giving in these instances to spouses, friends, and family under the guise of asking their advice.

Consider this scenario: "Can I ask your advice about something? I have an opportunity to paint a mural. Is it a stupid idea, or should I do it?"

You are not asking advice at all; you are asking permission.

How about this scenario: "A spot has opened up at a concert next week, but I am just too busy. Should I say yes or forget it?"

Again, you are a grown adult asking someone else if you should do something creative, fun, and slightly dangerous.

Without consciously understanding that we no longer need to ask anyone's permission, we are often stuck waiting for the universe to give us a sign, or we ask people around us for their blessing.

It might sound silly, but I find the easiest way to permit myself to do something is to write a permission slip. You know the little sheets of paper they used to give out in school?

Every student would need to ask for permission to go to the bathroom or leave to go to the principal's office. If caught in the corridor without a permission slip, you were in deep trouble. That flimsy little piece of paper held tightly in your hands was a free pass down the halls.

Even though you are grown up now, it is easy to conjure up that feeling of doing something naughty; being somewhere you shouldn't. You are doing something without permission. What will happen if you get caught? We never really take the time to think through these consequences. Who is the "they" who will catch you? What hallway monitors are in your life, checking on you and making sure you have permission to be here?

Once you understand that subconscious permission-programming is controlling your thoughts and behaviours, it can be quite terrifying to realise that it was actually you keeping yourself small.

The bad news, now that you know this, is that you have to do all the fun, creative, and dangerous things you were putting off. Clearing your brain of permission-programming makes way for decision-making. It is time to decide what you want to permit yourself to do.

Often this is the magic question. When you clear the permission-block, you become aware that you were using it as a handy crutch to avoid making decisions.

Permitting yourself is only one part of today's activity. You are also deciding what exciting, fun, and dangerously creative thing you would like to do if only you were allowed.

15-minute daily activity

Grab your pen and notebook, find a quiet place away from prying eyes and write a list of all the fun, creative, and dangerously exciting things you would do, if only you had permission to do them.

Choose one of them and write yourself a permission slip.

Access the free Creative Space bonus course and download your permission slip here: creativespace.link/course

Clear Creative Blocks

"Blocks usually stem from fear of being judged"—Erica Jong

Creative blocks are built by our brains to keep us safe

One of the biggest obstacles you will face when embarking on any self-improvement is your own brain. The amygdala is the part of the brain programmed to keep you safe at all costs, and this means finding ways to stop you doing dangerous things; such as being creative.

Back in the days of sabre-tooth tigers, avoiding danger was probably a plus for the survival of the species. Today, however, there isn't much out there which threatens your safety in the same way, so your amygdala will sabotage you from doing anything it sees as a threat to your current state and keep you in your comfort zone.

Over the years, humans have developed sophisticated methods of self-sabotage, and we can usually talk ourselves out of doing what will benefit us in the long run, in exchange for comfort now. The brain is an incredible asset when appropriately used, but it can also trick us if we don't understand it.

Some common ways humans self-sabotage include: overthinking, over-planning, perfectionism, distraction and procrastination.

However your creative blocks show up; your best work will only get done if you can clear out the saboteurs from your mind.

Cultivating an awareness of how fear plays a role in your life is essential if you are going to spend some time outside your comfort zone. Clearing blocks and protecting yourself against sabotage is also necessary if you are going to clear your mind for creativity.

Once you successfully negotiate with your amygdala and clear your creative blocks, it is possible to access the subconscious mind in ways which expand your creativity.

Take tiny imperfect action steps

When faced with a creative block, the answer is always the same; find ways to take tiny imperfect action steps towards your goal.

You can clear overthinking and over-planning blocks by taking action. It is impossible to steer a parked car. Just get moving and promise yourself you will course-correct as you go.

Perfectionists are surprised when you tell them this is also a creative block. We learn that perfectionism is a desirable trait, but the fear of making something less than perfect keeps many creatives stuck. There is also a paralysis to launch or release something because it is not perfect yet. As marketing guru Seth Godin says, "just keep shipping."

A less-than-perfect product out in the world can be improved upon over time based on user feedback. A less-than-perfect product hidden away in your computer or bedroom dies a sad and lonely death.

Distraction and procrastination manifest themselves in similar ways; we either do nothing, or something else more exciting, as a way to avoid the thing that blocks us.

If you are an overthinker or over-planner, you tend to do nothing other than talk or plan what you are going to do, so tiny imperfect action steps get you moving.

If you are a perfectionist, getting used to letting things go and releasing work that is less than perfect can also be helped by taking tiny imperfect action steps towards finishing and publishing your work.

If you are a procrastinator, breaking your mammoth tasks down into tiny action steps will also help. Instead of avoiding huge tasks for days and feeling guilty, eat the elephant one bite at a time.

If you are constantly distracted by shiny objects and newer, more exciting projects, slowing down your pace and doing less is the answer. Make your action steps smaller and keep them focused on the path.

15-minute daily activity

Over-thinkers and over-planners, what is one small action step you can take on a project you have been thinking about for years? If you are planning an exhibition, book a date in your calendar to work towards. If you are going to write a book "one day", start with 600 words today.

Perfectionists, what is one project you are still not happy with but it is 80% finished? Ship it. Get it out there. Give it to the people who need it. Get some feedback and then work on improving it.

Procrastinators, what mammoth, cumbersome task have you been putting off for weeks or even months? Write down every single tiny step involved in getting it done. If you have a list of five small steps, schedule each step over the next five days. If it is 30 steps, schedule each one for 30 days. Doing something tiny towards it is better than feeling guilty about not doing it.

Constantly distracted creatives (CDCs), pick ONE project for this month ... just one. You can always do something else next month. What are 30 tiny steps you can take on this one creative path? Hold yourself accountable for 30 days on one project and then review it after a month.

Prioritise Your Creativity

*"Most of us spend too much time on what is urgent
and not enough time on what is important"*—*Stephen Covey*

Putting others first often means putting your creativity last

Following on from the idea that we are conditioned to ask for permission, there is also social conditioning which trains us to put other people's needs first.

Opening doors for people, only speaking when spoken to, fetching and carrying for adults; these are all wonderful lessons to teach us respect and responsibility as children. However, as adults, putting other people first continues to influence our behaviour. It manifests itself as getting the kids ready for school, responding to urgent emails, saying "yes" when asked to do something for someone, and so on.

These are all examples of prioritising other people. Under the guise of politeness, respect, and responsibility, society conditions us to always put other people's needs before our own.

This system works if your to-do list for others is manageable. If you can work through all the needs and requests of others by lunchtime and still have time for yourself, then, by all means, go ahead and put their needs first.

However, most busy working people spend all day and often into the night working through their to-do list of other people's priorities (OPP) and rarely get through it all. The modern-day workplace and the invention of email enable a firehose of OPPs.

Even if you don't have kids and a full-time job, getting it all done is often impossible and time for yourself is the first thing to suffer.

Learn how to prioritise your creativity

In this day and age, the methods of prioritising that worked for our parents (and grandparents) no longer work for us. There is much more other people need us to do, and so many more ways they can get us to do it.

It is time to overcome your politeness-programming and set some boundaries in your day.

Learning to accept that you will never get it all done and learning instead to prioritise your own needs over the needs of others are two essential skills you will need to develop to claw back more time for yourself every day.

I am not going to lie to you—overcoming a lifetime of politeness-programming is difficult. Saying "no" feels rude, and the people in your life won't like it.

By working with a tool like the Priority Matrix, you can analyse all of the tasks, opportunities, requests and "someday" activities. You will never get everything done, so learning how to prioritise effectively is a modern-day skill everyone needs to develop.

An "Action Priority Matrix" is a simple diagram to help you choose the activities you should prioritise and the ones you should avoid, especially if you want to make the most of your limited time and precious energy.

The way it works is straightforward. A priority matrix is a simple grid with four quadrants. Along the left axis, it says "high impact" at the top and "low impact" across the bottom. Along the bottom axis, it has "low effort" on the left and "high effort" on the right.

The top left quadrant is a high impact, low effort activity. These are "quick wins" and you should focus on doing as many of these as possible.

The bottom left quadrant is a low impact, low effort activity. These are "fill-ins" and you should only do these types of tasks if you have spare time.

The top right quadrant is a high impact, high effort activity. These are "major projects" and you should focus on doing one of these at a time as they crowd out all the other activities.

The bottom right quadrant is a low impact, high effort activity. These are "thankless tasks" and you should focus on avoiding as many of these as possible.

15-minute daily activity

Grab a large sheet of paper and divide it into four quadrants. Label the top left "quick wins" bottom left "fill-ins" top right "major projects" and bottom right "thankless tasks."

Next, grab a stack of post-it notes and write every single task you have to do for yourself, or others, on a single post it. As you write each task, stick the post-it in the appropriate quadrant.

Everything you have placed in the bottom right "thankless tasks" quadrant, cease doing immediately. Delegate it if you have to, but concentrate on getting them off your to-do list.

Everything you have placed in the top left "quick wins" quadrant, focus on getting as many of these done each day as you can.

Everything you have placed in the top right "major project quadrant" decide which one takes priority and put the rest on the back-burner.

Only work on one major project at a time.

Everything you have placed in the bottom left "fill-ins" quadrant, only complete those if you finish your quick wins and significant projects for the day.

Access the free Creative Space bonus course and download your priority matrix here: creativespace.link/course

Learn to Forgive Yourself

*"Mistakes are always forgivable
if one has the courage to admit them"—Bruce Lee*

Creativity involves making mistakes

If you went through a traditional education system, chances are you have a clear distinction between giving a "right" answer and a "wrong" answer.

Traditional education systems praise the correct solution and discourage mistakes. It can be challenging then, to move into a creative headspace where mistakes are actively encouraged.

At all but the most progressive of schools, it is uncool to show a desire to learn, moreover challenge to status quo. Instead, teachers ask and reward students for the "right answer." As a result, being "wrong" is something humans usually try and avoid.

To be creatively successful, however, you must shift from a desire to validate your talent and intelligence to stretching to learn something new. This means being prepared to make mistakes.

As a society, we praise talent over hard work. Creatives must shift instead to valuing experimentation over always being right.

If left unchecked, it is possible to waste months of mental energy over-thinking mistakes. Without the ability to forgive yourself, you never truly move forward. Even after "solving" a thing you might have done "wrong" you will still carry the guilt of making a mistake in the first place. It is not uncommon to feel stupid and punish yourself for it with negative thoughts.

Without tolerance for mistakes and a desire to fail frequently, you will never be free to experiment or grow fully.

Learning to forgive yourself is the answer

It might come as a surprise to you, but mental punishment is just as destructive and painful to the psyche as physical punishment.

Making mistakes is unavoidable when trying new things. Mistake-avoidance is not a solution for creativity or growth; learning to forgive yourself quickly is.

You might never dream of physical aggression towards yourself, or others. The thought probably repulses you. Yet you might "beat yourself up" mentally for all your "stupid" mistakes, instead of celebrating and embracing them as signs of growth and progress.

The way to stop beating yourself up mentally, and clear out all those negative thoughts, is to connect the mental with the physical.

Whenever I hear somebody admonish themselves in a creative setting, I ask them to wear an elastic band around their wrist and snap it painfully. It causes much laughter and confusion at first, but if you snap that band against your wrist every time you beat yourself up, mentally or verbally, your wrist can become red raw by the end of the day.

This tool serves two purposes. It highlights the pain and damage you are doing to your psyche every time you beat yourself up. It also makes you painfully aware of how often you are thinking negative thoughts, and so you can begin the process of replacing those thoughts with positive ones.

15-minute daily activity

Today's activity is straightforward. Grab yourself a nice thick flat rubber band and wear it around your wrist.

Every time you think negative thoughts, beat yourself up, tell yourself it is a stupid idea, or call yourself an idiot, snap that band against the inside of your wrist—nice and hard—enough to leave a sting.

Keep it up for a few days and see how painful your poor wrist feels. Try and stop thinking negative thoughts, because this is precisely what you are doing to your psyche. Eventually, you can replace negative thoughts with positive ones and focus on forgiving yourself for every creative mistake you make.

Harness the Power of Fresh Starts

'The beginning is always today"—Mary Shelley

Every day is a fresh start

Why is the beginning of a new year so popular for making resolutions and fresh starts? What is it about a new year that brings up the resolve to take out gym memberships, start diets, and quit smoking? Why can't we harness this energy every day?

We also use the new year as a chance to reflect. Many people write long letters to the family as a wrap-up to their year. We look back at the highs and lows; we reflect on what happened, and this informs how we look forward to the future and all that the new year will bring. We also try and go on a holiday over these break periods as a way to restart the refresh the new work year as well.

The sad truth about new year's resolutions is the fresh start energy only lasts a few days. A feeling of failure is what stalls any creative program—to resolve to start again once a year is not enough.

By taking the time to understand your natural energy cycles, you can learn how to replenish your energy before you give up.

Unfortunately, humans don't come with a built-in energy gauge. A little dashboard light doesn't go on when it is time to fill up with fuel. You need to monitor your energy levels and fill them up daily.

The good news is, we can utilise shorter cycles as a way of kickstarting our motivation for change. Monthly, weekly and daily milestones are a useful catalyst to remind us to restore our energy.

Treating every day as a fresh start is a great way to stay motivated and on track.

The Fresh Start Effect

Professor Katherine Millman from the University of Pennsylvania researches something she calls the Fresh Start Effect. She describes how temporal landmarks, i.e. birthdays, holidays, new years, exist as a way to motivate aspirational behaviour.

Professor Millman talks about the power of harnessing milestones such as Mondays, public holidays or the start of every month. She argues that adding these milestones to our lives gives us regular moments to generate the same kind of new creative drive and energy that the start of a new year does.

Think of every new day as an opportunity to have a fresh start, every week, and every month. You can also have quarterly goals and review them once every three months throughout the year to get yourself back on track.

A creative renewal routine is the best way to ensure you don't just run dry with little warning.

The first step is to observe. What gets you energised and excited? What drains you? Do people, tasks or situations drain, or energise you? What experiences do you get a buzz out of and which ones make you groan?

Start paying attention to your energy levels as they fluctuate throughout your day.

An energy audit allows you to identify how you are feeling on an hourly basis, to gauge when and where you are most productive and most able to tackle difficult tasks. It can be quite revolutionary to work out that some tasks need focused energy, and others are low energy tasks, yet we tend to tackle them in the wrong order.

List the types of tasks you are regularly required to do and when you prefer to do them.

Adjust your daily schedule. Most people have higher energy levels in the morning, but until we are aware of how precious energy is, we don't realise it needs careful management. As a result, we drain valuable morning energy by checking emails as soon as we get to work, scheduling meetings at 10.30 am, putting off difficult tasks until the end of day and allowing social media to distract us.

This is known as a reactionary workflow, and it whittles away your best energy. It is unproductive and quite frankly, exhausting.

Schedule difficult tasks at times of the day when you know your energy levels are highest. Leave reactionary tasks, such as checking emails for when your energy is at its lowest.

If you work in an office, set a regular timer to get up and walk around. You might listen to a podcast on your morning commute to work and then read an inspirational book during your lunch break.

Establish some routines and rituals around injecting little bursts of energy activities into every day, every week, every month.

A daily exercise routine, even if it is just a 20-minute walk in the afternoon, can help refresh your energy reserves.

15-minute daily activity

Start harnessing the power of temporal milestones such as Mondays, the start of every month, and quarterly reviews as a way to get your goals back on track and renew your energy levels towards a challenging major project.

Quarterly

Start with a quarterly review. What do you want to achieve in the next three months? What do you want less of in your life? List the events which derailed your plans last quarter. What are some strategies you are going to try to be more focused and on-track in the next quarter?

Monthly

Break your quarterly plan down into months. If your major goal is to lose weight, what is your first monthly target? If your project is to write a book, how many words should you aim for in month one, two, and three?

When you get to the end of each month, take some time to restore your energy and review how you went. Try not to beat yourself up if month one didn't go according to plan. Review your goals and the steps you are taking and renew your energy for a fresh start to month two.

Weekly

Weekly goals work the same way. Look at your quarterly goal and your monthly goal. Break the monthly goal into four; these become your weekly targets. Use the same strategy when you conduct a weekly review. Sunday nights are great for these. Review what derailed you in the previous week. Update your strategy for the coming week and revise your goals. Take a weekly break to renew your energy and treat every Monday as a weekly fresh start.

Daily

Daily fresh starts. A nightly review can help you get back on track. Review what derailed your plans throughout the day and revise your goals for tomorrow. Remember to take daily energy breaks and journal every morning to start each day off with a fresh start.

Access the free Creative Space bonus course and download your fresh start template here: creativespace.link/course

Banish Energy Vampires

*"Say goodbye to the energy vampires in your life
(the negative souls who steal your enthusiasm)"—Robin Sharma*

Energy is precious, and these people will steal it from you

The previous six chapters of this book have shown you strategies to clear space in your brain for creativity. You have replaced negative thoughts with positive ones. You have prioritised what is most important, and you have harnessed the magic of fresh starts.

Now is the time to protect your fresh energy and clear headspace. There are those in your life who will seek to drain your new-found energy. They want to fill your clear head with their problems instead.

These are people who will regularly call you to whinge or vent. After the phone call, they feel better, but you feel drained. These people are energy vampires. If left unchecked, a weekly visit from an energy vampire can undo all of the great work you have done over the last few days.

Disclaimer: if someone calls to speak to you about a serious problem, by all means, take the call. Friends or family with genuine needs or issues are not energy vampires.

An energy vampire is someone who makes a regular energy withdrawal from you and gives nothing back in return.

Banish all energy vampires from your life

As harsh as it sounds, removing energy vampires from your life is the only solution.

Think of the people you currently interact with. When you see them or hear from them, does the interaction light you up or deflate you? Are you energised or drained by the conversation? When the phone rings and you see it is them, do you feel excited to take the call, or do you inwardly groan?

Your interactions with people should energise you, or at least leave you feeling neutral. It is not possible to get your best work done if others drain your precious energy and fill your head with their problems.

You must guard and protect your creative energy as fiercely as if you were protecting a child from harm, which means shifting the way you interact with energy vampires or cutting them off completely.

Here's the problem. They won't like it. Anyone who has come to rely on you as an energy source will not enjoy having it taken away.

The two strategies at your disposal are avoidance and dissipation.

If there is a place where you know you will likely encounter an energy vampire, avoid going there or change your routines and habits, so you go at different times. If they call you, don't take the call. If you are expected to call them, craft a way to change the expectation.

If avoidance is difficult, in a workplace, for example, try and engineer situations where there are more people around, and steer them towards group settings. More people means multiple conversations and opportunities to deflect the energy vampire.

Some strategies might be, if you regularly take a lunch break with an energy vampire, invite more people to join you, or move to the staff room where there are likely to be other people. Instead of meeting your friend for coffee, ask them round to dinner and invite other people as well.

Look for opportunities to shift the energy exchange and avoid one-on-one interactions with your energy vampires where possible.

15-minute daily activity

- » Write a list of all the people with whom you regularly interact.
- » Note beside each person an up arrow, down arrow, or equal sign.
- » The objective is to record whether interacting with them typically leaves you feeling energised, drained, or neutral.
- » Anyone with a down arrow next to their name is an energy vampire and must be banished. Write a list of typical scenarios where you might interact with them.
- » Look at the people and scenarios you have listed and brainstorm ways you can avoid or dissipate their energy-draining activities.
- » Put these strategies into practice over the next few weeks and months.

Access the free Creative Space bonus course and download your energy vampire template here: creativespace.link/course

CALENDAR SPACE

*In this section, you will learn how to steal time back from your day
and clear space in your calendar for creativity. You will discover how
to schedule in the margins of your day and set up systems to be more
productive. You will learn to say no to things and focus on your one thing.
You will uncover the power of tiny tasks and develop productive habits.*

Steal Back Your Own Time

*"All we have to decide is what to do with
the time that is given us"—J. R. R. Tolkien*

Time blocks mask other creative blocks

No matter who you talk to, not having enough time is always listed
as one of the top three reasons why something cannot be done.

"I'd love to write a book, but I don't have the time."

"I'd like to start a business, but I work forty hours a week."

*"I wish I had more time to practice the guitar, but the kids take priority
when I am at home."*

Allowing time to block your creativity is easy to justify. Everyone
you talk to will reinforce this block. No one has "time" to do fun
things if they have responsibilities. This is why it is easy to talk
about doing things "one day" as if a sabbatical will magically appear
and give you weeks of free time to write that book finally.

Here's the thing. For many of us, the delicious block of "free
time" never appears. If it does magically appear, such as during
coronavirus lockdown, it is still difficult to "find the time" to be
creative for a variety of reasons.

For the lucky few who make quality time-off a reality, the pressure to create something amazing can be debilitating, or they end up using the time to recharge instead.

How many people book a five-day cruise or go on holiday with big plans for a big project and wind up lying by the pool instead? There is nothing wrong with that. Your body uses those "all stop" moments to rest and recharge.

Time-creep is another problem we all face. It is the way very busy people still manage to spend seven hours a week on social media. It is how busy people can binge-watch an entire season on Netflix. It is how busy people can spend a Friday night drinking with friends after working all day.

When the activity is fun, distracting and engineered to be addictive, it is easy to lose track of time. It is easy to underestimate how much time we spend on these kinds of activities, especially when we are too tired to do anything "productive."

So how is it that some people with forty-hour day jobs still manage to start a business? How is it that people still get books written and pictures painted, even if they have kids and careers and lives just as busy as yours?

Here's the bad news. Your book, business, exhibition, guitar practice is more likely to get done during your busy workday than it is during a mythical block of "free time." Stealing time back is the only way successful busy creatives get things done.

Stealing time is the solution

Once you set clear priorities and identify the time-creeps in your day, you can steal back all the time you need.

Now before you start panicking that I am going to be the fun police, and take away your booze and Netflix, if you do this correctly, there will still be time for fun, relaxing activities, as well as attending to all of your responsibilities. You can also finish that major creative project you have been putting off due to not having enough time.

Sounds too good to be true? Let's look at the method.

Step one is to identify where your time goes. If the activities you do are measurable, such as watching three episodes of the Witcher on Netflix, you know that's three hours. If you turn on screen time on your iPhone, it will measure how long you spend on social media.

Think back over the last week and write down everything you remember doing. Did you visit a coffee shop every morning? How long are your lunch breaks? How much time do you spend watching TV or playing games every night? What did you do on the weekends? Identify all of the times where time-creep typically occurs.

The point of this exercise is to demonstrate to people who believe they are genuinely too busy to take on a creative project that there are many more hours in the day than you might think. Once you know where snippets of time are hiding, you can steal them back and stitch them together.

Step two is to identify what project you would like to undertake and then quantify it, so you know how much time you need to steal.

For example, if your dream is to one day write a book, work out how many words are in your book, let's say 60,000? That means that if you wrote 600 words every day, you would have your book written in four months. Once you get flowing, you can easily write 600 words in an hour.

If stealing back an hour is too difficult, how about 30-minutes in the morning and 30-minutes in the evening? That's easy if you already have a coffee habit in the morning. Take a notebook or iPad with you to the coffee shop and aim to write three pages. How do you think I managed to write this book and still work 40+ hours?

If your goal is to improve your guitar playing, how many hours practice do you need? If endless hours of training are impossible and let's face it, boring, why not practice a three-minute song three times a day? That's one full hour per week practising the same song 21 times.

Imagine how much you would improve if you practised one song 84 times in a month?

If the guitar is within arms reach, maybe play a song during every commercial while you are watching TV with the kids? Find ways to keep it accessible and chip away at your practice time. Maybe the kids can help out with a percussive accompaniment?

If your creative goal is to start a business, you need to schedule decent blocks of time throughout the week. Try and batch your tasks so that all the computer activities get done on the weekend. Maybe watching courses can be done at night on the couch and make all your phone calls in your lunch breaks?

Step three is to work with your calendar to see where you can steal time back, and be prepared to take action whenever blocks of time are "gifted" to you. You will be amazed by what you can get done if you are prepared.

I have written three books in my lunch breaks—600 words at a time. I painted a series of portraits by getting to work half an hour earlier and keeping the paints hidden in my desk drawer. I have journaled every day for 15 years by writing in my notebook with my morning coffee. I have taught myself many skills by watching YouTube videos on the couch in the evenings and listening to podcasts on my daily commute. What could you do with snippets of time stolen back from your day?

15-minute daily activity

Brainstorm a list of things you wish you had more "time" to do.

Check your weekly calendar and identify any typical time-creep sessions. When do you find yourself "wasting time" or spending more time on an activity than you need to? These are usually leisure activities but can often be procrastination times or work breaks.

Instead of chatting away your lunch breaks or spending time on your phone, what could you do for half an hour that is productive and builds towards your dream?

Set a goal to steal back 30-minutes tomorrow and do something creative with the time. Plan out what you are going to do now. You can still mindlessly scroll Instagram and watch Netflix. You only need to reclaim 30-minutes per day.

Here are some ideas. Bring a notebook to work and sketch in it at lunchtime. Download a course and watch it on the couch at night. Read a book on your kindle app while the kids have basketball practice. Listen to a useful podcast or audiobook on your commute to work. Write 600 words on your phone while waiting for your morning coffee. The Paper app by Dropbox is my favourite tool.

Work with your rhythm and flow throughout the day. Plan ways to steal time and be prepared for any opportunity to capitalise on any unexpected time gifts. There is nothing worse than waiting 20-minutes for a friend who is running late and not having a notebook on you.

Use these time gifts to read or write something productive instead of wasting it on your phone. Keep headphones in your bag so you can watch a course or instructional video instead.

Be prepared to steal time daily and outline a list of ways to use that time productively.

Harness the Power of Tiny Tasks

"When eating an elephant,
take one bite at a time"—Creighton Abrams

How do you eat an elephant?

As our lives become busier, we tend to rely heavily on to-do lists. They are great if used properly, but it can be challenging to allocate the right amount of time to each list item. It also becomes a procrastination nightmare if some of the tasks are too big.

The very nature of a list means that all items appear equal and it is only when moved to the top something becomes prioritised.

Consider these two list items:

» Email Frank about the meeting
» Do your tax return.

Emailing Frank is easy and will probably take two minutes. Doing your tax return will take hours, maybe days and involves many steps and processes. It might also include other people's input.

The problem arises when you don't know what is involved in a to-do list item, so it is endlessly pushed to the bottom of the list, or the next day, depending on how you work your lists.

The other issue, even if you do manage to scope large projects properly, is that while you become immersed in one project, all the steps and stages involved with another project get forgotten.

Ever get three-quarters of the way through a significant project only to have another project appear and take priority? When you finally get back to the first project, it can take hours, even days to get back up to speed with where you were at with it.

One bite at a time

The solution to all of these problems is simple. Break every single project down into tiny tasks; 15-minutes at the most. Your first task for every major project on your to-do list should be to scope the project down into all the tiny tasks.

Once you have listed all the tiny tasks involved in each project, you can schedule one or two every day. This way, your procrastination brain can deal with the tiny chunks. You also move all of your projects along concurrently, which means you stay "in it" and don't waste precious time or energy getting up to speed on things.

It also means that every single item on your to-do list does have equal weighting. Emailing Frank and emailing your accountant are equally weighted tasks and just as quick and easy.

By emailing your accountant today and finding your box of receipts tomorrow and sorting through the receipts on Friday, you are using a series of tiny tasks to move you through the enormous task of doing your tax. By the end of the week, you are five steps closer to finishing the project you have been procrastinating on for weeks.

I have experimented with many paper and digital tools over the years. None works better with the tiny tasks method than Todoist.

The reason I like Todoist is you can create projects out of all of your big tasks, such as writing a book, renovating the kitchen, planning an exhibition, and so on. Then you can list under each project all the steps, or tiny tasks.

These lists can become very large, as you might imagine, but by only scheduling the next three or four days, you keep the rest of the tasks hidden from your daily list until it is time to deal with them.

You can also make items recurring, such as going to the gym three days a week or scheduling your newsletter every Thursday.

By scheduling a tiny task every day for each of your major projects, you can move them along and still intersperse your other daily tasks as they arise.

15-minute daily activity

The goal of this exercise is to break down your projects into a
sequence of tiny tasks. A tiny task must be able to be done in one
sitting, take 15-minutes or less, be clear, and easy to tick off.

Download Todoist (or something similar) onto your phone, tablet,
or computer. Start by drafting a list of all your major and minor
projects on the left-hand side. You can nest projects if you like.
Create a project which is for recurring tasks, such as gym days or
weekly reminders.

Your first tiny task for every project is to scope the project into
tiny tasks. It can be difficult to see too far ahead with a project, so
list out as many of the next fun and easy steps as you can. You can
project the following phases as you move further down the path.

Once you have listed your significant projects and the first few
tiny steps for each, schedule the next three days. You do this by
working down the list of projects, take the first 15-minute tiny task
in each project and schedule it for tomorrow. You can then view the
calendar for the next seven days, and you will see all the tiny tasks
you need to do tomorrow.

Urgent quick tasks will arise daily, so add these to your day using
the inbox feature, or make another project called daily tasks.

Schedule them as they occur, and they will appear on the daily list, along with your other projects.

Remember to use the same tiny task method for every new project or activity.

If something occurs to you at the time, like registering for a conference, you can do it in under 15-minutes, so add it to your daily list. If you are not sure which conference you want to attend, though, that might be two tiny tasks.

One Todoist item is to research three conferences online and then the second Todoist item is to grab your credit card and register for the conference. Both can be done in under 15-minutes.

Don't be tempted to clump a couple of tiny tasks together. Procrastination rears its ugly head when we overload our to-do lists.

Schedule in the Margins

*"Margin is the space between our load
and our limits"—Richard Swenson*

Calendars can often get hijacked

Whether you work at a large organisation or by yourself, your calendar is often at the mercy of other people. Appointments, meetings, and all forms of scheduled activity can hijack your day, or even your week.

What is often worse is the time wasted in between meetings. If you run from one appointment to another and the break between isn't large enough to do anything productive, the whole day can become a washout if you are not prepared.

You have probably heard this story before, but the rocks, pebbles, sand, analogy works well when it comes to an understanding of how calendar time works.

A teacher stands in front of a classroom and starts putting rocks in a jar. Once the jar is full, she asks the students if she can fit in any more. They all reply no.

She then gets some tiny pebbles and proceeds to pour them in between the rocks in the jar. She asks the class again, is the jar full. Most of them reply, yes. Some have started to switch on.

She then fills the jar with sand, which moves in between the pebbles and the rocks.

Now the jar is full.

If you approach your calendar the same way, you can see that even though you fill your week with meetings and appointments (rocks), you can still load the gaps with smaller tasks (pebbles) and then in between those, even more, minor tasks (sand).

I often keep a list on my phone of annoying little tasks that can be done quickly in between large rocks, or meetings. I also carry my journal everywhere so I can write Morning Pages if a session finishes early. These are examples of the pebbles in the teacher's jar demonstration.

Even smaller tasks might be ten star-jumps or drinking a glass of water, or meditating for a few minutes. These are tiny little tasks that don't mean much on their own, but remembering to do them in the margins of time between the rocks and pebbles means you can get a lot more done than your calendar would suggest.

Block out your rocks, pebbles, and sand

Coffee dates, hairdressing appointments, trips to the gym, and school pickups should all go on your calendar, as well as work meetings, client calls, and so on. Remember to add travel time on the calendar as well. Commuting to work as well as travelling between shops or buildings should all be added.

Make sure all of your rocks are in the jar before you start adding in the pebbles.

Start planning the tiny tasks you can do in the gaps, as well as being prepared if meetings finish early. Carry your journal with you, maybe an iPad so you can get some tasks done on the go.

You might want to call these "pebble tasks" to help clarify that they are not sand and they are not rocks. Tiny tasks are 15-minutes or less, so make sure you carry your Todoist app with you and tick off tiny tasks in the gaps.

The final stage is to draft a list of quick habits you would like to improve. Many people want to drink more water, stretch, or take a few minutes to meditate.

Carry a list on your phone, or better still, download a habits app and then in those minutes between meetings, you can be reminded to stand and stretch, or close your eyes for a three-minute chair meditation, or go fill up your water bottle, ready for your next meeting.

The key to getting more out of your day is by preparing for it. Place the rocks in your calendar, fill your Todoist with pebble tasks and start a sand-filled habits list.

15-minute daily activity

As you move through your busy week, think of your appointments as rocks, your tiny tasks as pebbles and your daily habits as sand.

Rocks

Spend some time planning your week by placing all the appointments in your calendar first. You can use any calendar app on your phone or whatever you already use for work appointments.

Pebbles

You should already have the Todoist app filled with tiny tasks, but if you don't, draft a list of easy 15-minute tasks that need doing.

Sand

Download a habit app to your phone, such as Habit—Daily Tracker. Fill it with mini-tasks or habits you'd like to tick off during the day.

Fill in the gaps between your stones with pebble tasks and sand habits and see how much more you get done this week.

Access the free Creative Space bonus course and see examples of rocks, pebbles, and sand scheduling here: creativespace.link/course

Learn to Say No

"Real freedom is saying 'no' without a reason"—Amit Kalantri

Saying yes to one thing means saying no to something else

We learn to be polite. We learn to be accommodating. Unfortunately, this often means we often end up saying yes to things we don't want to do.

Have you ever found yourself agreeing to a trivia night, or a parent-teacher evening, or standing in for somebody at a sporting match? As you sit there and look around, you wonder how exactly you came to be here and why you aren't at home right now doing something more productive?

This is because nice, polite people don't say "no" very often. We don't want to hurt people's feelings; we don't want to be difficult. Unfortunately, in this busy day and age, saying "yes" to something means saying "no" to something else.

Worse than saying yes because we don't want to appear awkward, is saying yes and then feeling guilty for saying no later. It is better to

---

have a little awkwardness now rather than disappointing someone down the track.

Look at all the hard work you did stealing time back in the previous module, only to have it snatched back from you because you can't say no.

The other problem that makes a polite "no" even harder is that the offers which come your way can often sound pretty good. However, "pretty good" doesn't light you up. "Not bad" doesn't get your book written. "Just OK" is a waste of your time.

There is an opportunity cost of saying yes to things which are just OK. As bestselling author Derek Sivers says, it is either "HELL YEAH or No."

Build your No muscle

Learning to say no is like any other muscle. You can build up your no muscle with exercise. The more you do it, the better you get at it. The difficulty is not appearing rude, and even though no is a complete sentence, if you think you are going to struggle with this, you might want to have some other methods of declining invitations up your sleeve.

For example, "thank you so much for your lovely invitation to catch up with you over coffee, but I have scheduled all of my coffee dates for the next three months."

How about, "I appreciate the invitation to speak at your local charity evening, but I am currently focusing on writing my book. Good luck with your event."

A good fallback with in-person invitations is to say that you will get back to them after you have checked your calendar. This gives you enough time to think of a plausible excuse if you don't have the confidence to say no to their face.

The best method, however, is to learn how to say no without giving any reason or excuse. If accepting an invitation helps their agenda, but doesn't further yours, you should practice saying no. Firmly and politely.

The primary tool I use when I am undecided as to whether I should accept an invitation or opportunity is Derek Siver's hell yeah test. I ask myself, is this a hell yes opportunity? If it isn't, the answer is always no.

Do I want a free trip to Italy? Hell yes. Do I want to drive for 20-minutes to pick a friend up at the airport? Nope. Send them an Uber. Do I want to have dinner with Jason Momoa? Hell yes. Do I want to have dinner with my friend's parents? Not a chance.

It is the difference between doing something out of a feeling of obligation or duty, versus excitement and interest. Just because someone asks you to do something, that is not a good enough reason to say yes.

15-minute daily activity

Practice saying "no" to everything today.

If you are at work and a colleague says "do you want to get coffee?" Practice saying "no thank you" and then do something creative with the time instead.

If you are picking the kids up after school and one of the parents asks you to come over for dinner tomorrow, tell them you are fully booked at the moment. Then book the time you would have spent at dinner on your creative calendar.

Spend the rest of the week looking out for hell yes invitations and practice saying no to everything else, even if it sounds OK, or pretty good.

Remember. If it is not a hell yeah, the answer is no.

Build up that no muscle by learning to disappoint people slightly, then schedule the time you just rescued, for yourself.

Develop Productive Systems

*"We should work on our process.
Not the outcome of our processes"—W. Edwards Deming*

Repetitive tasks drain your energy

In our busy lives, we often find ourselves doing the same things over and over. Repetitive tasks can be energy-draining because we get no excitement or novelty from completing them. They also take time away from our day where we could be doing something creative.

The worst repeating tasks are those that only happen periodically, like every quarter. Whenever they come around, we have usually forgotten what we did last time and have to relearn or remind ourselves of the process every time.

You might realise at the time the activity is energy-draining, but it is often just quicker to complete it than spend time trying to systemise, automate, or delegate the task. However, as Abraham Lincoln was famously quoted as saying "Give me six hours to chop down a tree, and I will spend the first four sharpening the axe."

It takes some thought and effort to set up systems, sure, but the time and energy saved in the future make it worth the time and effort now.

Spend some time systemising tasks

Depending on the type of repetitive task, there are a variety of solutions. The ones we will look at for this activity are automation, delegation, and setting up systems and workflows.

Automation is where you use an app or digital service to do a task for you. The simplest one is automatically paying bills or topping up a savings account with wages. Most financial services offer an online banking service. If money is deposited into your account regularly, you can set it up to automatically move regular amounts of money into your savings accounts or bill accounts.

For example, if your phone or power bill arrives every quarter, but you get paid every fortnight, simply divide a typical quarterly statement by six and then arrange to have that amount deposited automatically every paycheck. Your bank will have to ability to set up recurring payments online.

This serves two purposes; the bill is paid automatically in advance, so you never get caught short. It also saves you time paying the bills.

Delegation is the next strategy to save time and energy. It is as simple as getting someone else to do it.

The primary reason I find busy creatives struggle to delegate is not that we can't find anyone to do the task. It is because we can't allow others to do things differently. If you are a control freak like I am, it is difficult to let go of the task.

Practice delegating a repetitive task, such as putting the bins out or doing the shopping and let go of the outcome. If there are weekly staples to buy, write a shopping list and delegate it to someone in your household.

Empower other members of your family to take on a weekly cooking schedule. Even if the best your ten-year-old can manage is baked beans on toast, let go of needing every meal to be perfect.

Taking this approach frees more time up for you and empowers those around you to take ownership of certain activities.

If you run your own business, you can delegate tasks for money. Hire a part-time bookkeeper to come in one day a week. Delegate repetitive tasks like posting to social media or following up with deliveries. It might cost money, but your time is worth more.

The third strategy is to develop systems and processes for all of your repetitive tasks and workflows. It might sound like a waste of time, but writing a list of all the steps involved in a complicated workflow saves you time later.

Firstly, having workflows means you don't need to expend any energy remembering the steps. Secondly, you don't miss any actions or get the steps confused. Thirdly, you can begin to delegate more processes to others when they are documented.

For example, every year, I produce a book of the best lettering in the world. Every December we put the call out for submissions. There are many steps involved in advertising the call-for-entries, processing the submissions, getting artist approval, making corrections, getting print quotes, sending it to print, processing pre-orders, and so on.

The book only happens once a year, so it is easy to forget the steps if I didn't have them written down. It saves me time and improves the quality if I just follow the workflow I wrote down the year before.

Processing receipts for lodging a tax return would fall into this same category. Any quarterly or yearly activity with multiple steps will benefit from a system or workflow.

There are multiple tools to assist you with repetitive tasks. If you have a smartphone or computer, there are free and paid apps. Your bank and supermarket can also supply you with automation tools and delivery options.

If it is human help you need, start with eLance or Fiverr where you can post a list of tasks you need and people will apply. You can also post to a local bulletin board or Facebook group. You might even know someone who could use five hours of part-time work a week.

15-minute daily activity

- » Write a list of your repetitive tasks and chores.
- » Divide them into daily, weekly, monthly, quarterly and yearly.
- » Work out if they can be automated, delegated, or systemised.
- » Practice one of each type. Set up automation with your bank for your household bills to start with.
- » Delegate something like posting to social media or content research to a virtual assistant for five hours a week.
- » Write a workflow for a complicated list of tasks such as lodging your tax return. Store it on Evernote or Dropbox Paper.

Focus on Your One Thing

"The key to success is to focus our conscious mind on things we desire, not things we fear"—Brian Tracy

Distraction is the enemy of productivity

Most creatives suffer from shiny object syndrome. It is only natural to be excited by new projects, especially when they are so full of promise and you are stuck in the messy middle of something else.

The problem with creative distractions is that we never finish what we start.

The creative stereotype paints us as flaky and self-indulgent, and this might be because we are forever dropping projects to pick up new ones. I am as guilty as the next person.

If you are not flaky and don't drop your current projects, something even worse is likely to happen. You become so exhausted juggling the nine things on your plate because creative distractions get added to your to-do list, alongside your current projects.

We learnt to say no to other people in a previous exercise. In this activity, we need to learn to say no to ourselves.

Every time I find myself getting excited about a new project, a new direction, a new idea, I remind myself of this quote:

"You can do anything you want. But you can't do everything."

Focus on one thing at a time

Before you start a new project, you must ask yourself "which project have I just finished, or will I shelve to make room for this project?"

If you haven't just finished a project or you can't pause something you are currently working on, then it is the new idea you need to shelve. You can always get to it later, once you clear something else off your plate.

The best way to get clarity and focus on every creative project is to understand what motivates you. Once you are grounded in your motivation, you can quickly pivot when an idea changes and evolves. You can go from flaky to focussed once you understand your bigger Why.

You might have already heard about Simon Sinek and his Start with Why book. Simon's TEDx talk is one of the most-watched talks on the TED website.

Simon's primary argument is that people don't buy what you do; they buy why you do it.

He also argues that most people can tell you what they do and even how they do it, but very few people can articulate why they do something.

As a business coach, his mission is to bring entrepreneurs and businesses into alignment with their Why, How, and What. He adds the proviso that you can pivot what you do or how you do it without changing your Why.

Simon cites Apple as an example of a company that continually pivots, from a computer company to a music delivery service, a smartphone provider, and so on. The motivation driving Apple stays the same through all these what and how changes; to challenge the status quo.

He gives the example of what a mission statement might look like from a Why-driven company like Apple:

> *"Everything we do, we believe in challenging the status quo. We believe in thinking differently. The way we challenge the status quo is by making our products beautifully designed, simple to use, and user-friendly. And we happen to make great computers. Wanna buy one?"*

Even though the examples he gives in his talk are related to big brands, you can easily transfer the concepts to your own life.

Simon introduces a tool in his talk called the Golden Circle. He draws a Why in the centre circle. How in the middle ring and What in the outside ring.

The idea is that if your Why anchor in the middle is strong enough, you can pivot your thoughts around it. Becoming clear on your Why gives you clarity and focus around what projects you should be doing and which ones you should shelve for now.

15-minute daily activity

Draw yourself a target with a middle circle and two outer rings. Write WHY in the middle, HOW in the second circle and WHAT in the outside ring.

Write down all of the things you like doing and how you do them. For example, writing instructional books might be HOW you do something and the WHAT is teaching people how to play the guitar.

Once you have a list of everything you do or would like to do, see if there is a common thread which drives them all. What is the motivation behind your creative pursuits?

Access the free Creative Space bonus course and download your golden circle template here:
creativespace.link/course

Develop Productive Habits

"Quality is not an act; it is a habit"—Aristotle

Old habits keep you stuck

We already know about bad habits, but even good habits may no longer be serving us. One of the keys to successful productivity, especially when we are super busy, is to have productive habits, and this means reviewing all of our habits periodically.

Habits are activities you do without consciously thinking about them. If an action is repeated often enough, it becomes housed in your subconscious. Some examples might be biting your nails, driving a car, riding a bicycle, scrolling your phone, brushing your teeth, flushing the toilet, and so on.

We only notice we are doing these things when something breaks the routine. For example, if the toilet flush doesn't work, or we run out of toothpaste. These consciousness breaks make us aware of the habit, and as soon as we fix the issue, we return subconsciously to the habit.

Many of your habits have been with you since early childhood, but driving a car or checking emails are habits learned later in life. When you learned how to drive, for example, you spent time consciously executing the steps until eventually your subconscious took over and the actions become habits. Now you can probably drive a car without thinking too much about it.

If it is possible to make all the complicated steps involved in driving a car or riding a bike become a habit, it is also possible to make productivity a habit. Consciously learning the steps involved in productive workflows until they become habits will save a wealth of time and energy.

Part of the process of cultivating new habits also means replacing unwanted habits. There is no such thing as a bad habit or a good habit. Think of them as habits you want and habits you don't want.

You developed your habits for a reason. If you decide they no longer serve you, you can consciously choose to replace them with other, more productive habits.

Make sure your habits are helpful

Developing and maintaining productive habits can initially take some conscious thought and effort, but the results are well worth it.

Using things you already do to trigger actions you want is an effective way to implement new habits.

If you want to listen to more podcasts or audiobooks, for example, use the habit of getting into your car to trigger a podcast selection on your phone.

If you want to read more books or articles, use the habit of reaching for your phone to open Medium or Kindle instead of Facebook or Instagram. Put the productive apps on your front screen and hide the distracting apps in a folder.

Once you have one habit firmly ingrained, you can use it to stack another. For example, if you want to floss your teeth every day, you can stack it on to the habit you already have of brushing your teeth.

I used to walk on the treadmill at the gym but found it boring. I also wanted to read more but could never "find the time." The solution was to stack one habit on top of the other. I would read books on my iPad while walking on the treadmill. I used to enjoy both activities much more by stacking them together, and I also cut the time to do both in half.

If you want to find more time to be creative, what habits can you stack or trigger to save time and also get more done?

You might use the strategy to get your work or household tasks done more efficiently to free up more spare time to be creative. Alternatively, you might stack or trigger your creative habits to ensure you get in some practice or time on the tools.

I wanted to improve my iPad lettering skills, for example, so I used my existing habit of relaxing after dinner to trigger an iPad practice session. I moved the iPad charging station so that it was near the couch, and this meant the iPad was always in reach. Every night now, when I slump down onto the sofa, I look over, and there is the iPad. Charged and waiting. All I need to do is pick it up and start practising. Using this habit trigger, I manage to get at least 20-minutes practice every night.

15-minute daily activity

Habit triggers are when you examine things you already do and use them to trigger a new habit. Observe throughout the day, something you always do habitually. What related activities could you remind yourself to do?

Habit stacking is where you add one habit to another—flossing while brushing; listening to podcasts while walking; or audiobooks while cleaning. Why not try singing while walking the dog? You get the idea.

Spend the day examining your habits. Write a list of things you would like to do if you had more time or willpower. Write a plan for how and where you can trigger or stack your new habits.

Practice throughout the day. It takes 66 days on average to develop a new habit, so don't worry if you forget or fall off the wagon now and then. Set a daily habit reminder on your phone and keep at it.

PHYSICAL SPACE

In this section, you will learn how to clear space for creativity. You will discover how to set up a studio, even if you don't have any space. You will learn how to set boundaries around your time and take creative breaks to recharge. You will uncover the magic of coffee shops and understand why getting control of your digital space is just as important as your physical space.

Clear Space for Creativity

*"The best way to find out what we really need
is to get rid of what we don't"—Marie Kondō*

Clutter is not conducive to creativity

There is a Facebook meme that says something like "A messy desk
is the sign of a creative mind."

Invariably a few friends will take ownership of this as a sign of
victory. Their messy lives and chaotic rooms now offered up as
validation of their creative mind, instead of a problem that needs
addressing.

If you look at both extremes—compulsive tidiness and hoarders—
there are psychological drivers behind both groups. A happy,
productive, well-balanced, creative life doesn't appear at either end
of this spectrum, but I am here to tell you, creativity needs clarity.

There needs to be physical and mental space for creativity to
flourish. Much like a garden where everything is allowed to
grow, eventually, the weeds will take over. Any seedlings and

delicate flowers will be strangled and suffocated. Your blossoming ideas need space to grow, which means a regular weeding of the unwanted.

If memories and worries crowd your brain or you find yourself remembering to remember things, then any fledging creative ideas will be shouted over and buried. If notes and thoughts and sketches need to find their way onto paper, and there is nowhere to sit and write, then these ideas may never see the light of day.

There is an old Shaker saying: "A place for everything, and everything in its place." This religious order is known for their clean and tidy spaces, to allow them the space to think clearly and get closer to God. The problem tends to arise when not everything has a place.

There are two types of mess. The first is a productive mess, where you found things stored away somewhere and made use of them. All that is needed to clear this kind of mess is to put things back where you found them.

The second type of mess is much harder to clear up. This is when new things have come into your house or workspace, and there isn't anywhere to put them.

Clear up your clutter

The solution to clutter involves four steps.

The first is to separate (and put away) things which already have a home. These tend to be kitchen utensils, plates, clothes, and toys.

The second step is to locate all the things which don't have a home yet and put them in one place, like the dining room table. These are usually papers, letters, and new purchases.

The third step involves sorting through the pile and throwing away anything you no longer need.

The fourth step consists of finding homes for all the new things you decided to keep. This might also entail the purchase of new storage or the repurposing of old storage.

You might also want to systemise the putting away of things so that they don't build up again, such as getting the kids to put away toys before bath-time or folding dry clothes in front of the television. Start a roster of people to take out the trash or empty bottles. Get into the habit of opening mail and putting it in a keep pile or a get rid of pile.

15-minute daily activity

Start with the place where you usually work. You can move on to another part of the house or workplace tomorrow and apply the same techniques.

» Put away everything which already has a place, in a cupboard or a drawer.
» Grab everything else in a pile on the floor or a table.
» Sort through what to throw away, and then throw it away.
» Decide what to do with the things you are keeping.
» Find homes for the new things, or clean out some old storage to make room.
» Develop systems to deal with the new stuff as it comes into the house.

Set up Your Studio

"To me, being in the studio is one of the most exciting parts about being an artist"—Jamie Lynn Spears

No creative space means no creative play

One of the biggest complaints I hear from creatives is the lack of studio space. If you are not lucky enough to have a studio or office space, it can be challenging to set up your tools.

Even if you do have a workplace or external studio, it can also be beneficial to have another workplace set up at home.

Often, however, it is not the lack of space which stops creativity at home; it is an external block. If you live with other people, housemates or family, there is a self-consciousness about taking over part of the house to be creative.

If, after looking through the suggestions for a home studio nook, you find yourself still making excuses, it might be time to have a frank discussion with the other people in your house.

Let them know you want to set up a study nook and get their input as to where the best place is from their perspective. By getting buy-in from your household, there is clarity about what you are doing. There might be some sympathy around the additional clutter in the house.

A studio can be a desk or a laptop

The first step to building your studio space anywhere is to let go of any spacious, airy studio dreams you might have lusted over in books and websites. It is possible, however, to create a study nook in just about any room, and Pinterest often has excellent small space ideas if you need inspiration.

I am lucky enough to have a custom-built studio now, but it took a $30,000 mortgage refinance and a handy hubby six months to complete. For the 30 years before that, I ran my illustration business from a combination of kitchen tables, couches, living room floors, garages, bedroom nooks, spare rooms, and coffee shops.

Once you shift your mindset about what a home studio has to look like, the solution might be as simple as grabbing a pen and a notebook and keeping it next to the couch or the bed.

It is possible to be creatively productive without any tools other than a laptop or a notebook. I know several freelance designers who work productively from their bed. All they need is a MacBook and an internet connection.

If you are a musician or a painter, or a lettering artist, you might need a few extra things. If finding room for a desk is impossible, a stable table and a storage box convert any couch or bed into a mini laptop studio.

Having your tools or instruments accessible is the most important thing to consider when planning a studio nook.

If what you need is waiting, right next to where you usually sit, it is much easier to noodle around and get something done every day. If you pack everything away in a cupboard, you are much less likely to go and grab everything out.

The best option is a dedicated table or workspace. Look at ways you can rearrange the furniture in your room to add a little table in the corner. IKEA has many solutions for small spaces available, and a few creative storage options mean you can convert the corner of a bedroom, balcony or living room into a studio desk.

Fishing tackle boxes make great portable tool kits. The lid opens up and displays all your tools neatly, then folds away again.

If there is room for a little table somewhere, on the deck, in the lounge room, or your bedroom, measure the space and order one.

TIP: desks for home are usually much cheaper than desks for an office when searching online.

Most fishing and outdoor shops have small fishing tackle boxes for putting away pens, brushes, and small craft items. Craft stores also have storage options, depending on your creative studio needs.

If you genuinely don't have room for a small table, then invest in a lap table of some sort. Office supplies stores have laptop platforms. You can place a larger board on top if you need room for sketching and drawing. Again, a fishing tackle box keeps tools within arms reach and is quick and easy to pack away.

15-minute daily activity

Write down all of your options for studio space and any potential obstacles. Discuss your options with your family or housemates if your plans impact their living space. Start small and be reasonable with your request.

Tidy the room and rearrange any furniture to make space for your new desk and chair. Measure the space accurately.

Go online and search for a tiny table (or laptop platform). Search also for some storage options, including a fishing tackle box.

If you buy a fishing tackle box, put all your pens and brushes in the little drawers and make sure it opens and closes easily.

When you have your bits and pieces, set up the studio space and keep it tidy. Make sure everything you need is within arms reach so you can sit down and start work right away.

The most important part of a studio space is having everything you need immediately available and set up all the time, ready to go when you are.

If you have a little more space available than just a portable lap-desk, add a few plants and pictures to make your study nook feel creatively inspiring. A studio needs to be inviting, no matter what size it is.

Establish Clear Boundaries

"Daring to set boundaries is about having the courage to love ourselves, even when we risk disappointing others"—Brené Brown

Distractions are the enemy of productivity

There are two types of distractions. The first is when you allow yourself to be interrupted, and the second is when other people interrupt you without your permission.

Let's look at self-interruption first. Most of these instances result from a lack of awareness or willpower.

Picking up your phone and checking notifications or visiting the fridge for a snack are great activities when you have worked solidly for 90-minutes, and you need a break. They are not so useful when you haven't settled down to work yet, or when you keep checking your phone without knowing why.

Another distraction we tend to allow is email. When you receive as many as I do, without some sort of boundaries set in place, I could sit in front of my computer responding to them all day.

People often complain that they have to be responsive to emails; it is their job. True, but unless you are in a call centre or customer support, your boss probably expects some other form of productivity from you as well. It helps to put boundaries in place around when you check and respond.

Task switching is another form of distraction. You can lie to yourself and call it multitasking but if you are trying to be creative or get some deep work done, give yourself some boundaries around how long you will focus on this task and turn everything else off.

People are the second type of distraction. At home, you might have kids, family, or neighbours who all need something from you at random moments throughout the day. At work, you might have coworkers, cleaners, security, or customers who all like to drop by for a chat.

The dreaded telephone allows anyone from anywhere to interrupt your workflow. It always makes me laugh when people ask "is this a good time to talk" when they call during work hours.

Every day is a minefield of distractions and interruptions, so to be productive, it helps to set some clear boundaries, with yourself, and those around you.

Battle distractions before they happen

Let's look at each of the problems one-by-one because each issue has a different solution.

Lack of awareness or willpower is a difficult one because you have to battle ingrained habits. Reaching for the phone every ten minutes is an unconscious habit that many people struggle with, myself included.

One trick is to turn all notifications off so that it doesn't buzz for your attention. Keep it face down or covered while you are working so you can't see any notifications, or better still, keep it in another room. Reward yourself with some phone and fridge time after every 90-minute concentration session.

This strategy also helps with task switching. Work out what tasks you need to give your full attention and then focus on one for 90-minutes straight. Then you can reward yourself with some quick wins or mundane tasks that require less focus.

The little "bing" sound that notifies you of yet another email landing in your inbox is one of the worst distractions of the modern era. Setting boundaries around email means only checking it at certain times throughout the day and turning off those annoying notifications.

I tend to check (and process) emails twice daily, once at 10:30 am, and again at 5 pm. That way, people feel responded to promptly, but I also build out some buffer time for myself before and after the 10:30 session to get more important work done.

Setting boundaries with other people can be a little harder, but often all it takes is a conversation or some thoughtful structure. Take some time to think about your preferred working hours and your downtime. Then discuss these times with your family.

I always need a break at around 3:30 pm as my energy levels dip. That's a great time for me to go for a walk with my husband or get the food shopping done. He used to come and interrupt me at all hours of the day when it occurred to him that we needed something from the supermarket. Now he knows that 3:30 pm is walk and shop time, he leaves me alone until then.

Routines can change, and not everything falls when you need it to, but if there is an opportunity to set some daily schedules with the people around you, at least have the discussion and iron out any bumps as they arise.

Setting boundaries at work can be a little harder, but not impossible. If you work in an open-plan office, wearing visible headphones can give a clear signal that you are not to be bothered right now.

If you are lucky enough to work in an office with a door, put office hours outside and refuse to answer the door if people knock outside of those times.

It might be a good idea to speak with your boss about scheduling meetings and deep work time throughout the week so that everyone is on the same schedule. Without guidelines and boundaries, people tend to run amok. If you can instigate a workplace-wide program, others might appreciate the clarity as well.

The final distraction is phone calls. If you have regular family phone calls, try and schedule them. I always call my husband during my lunch break, for example.

If you receive lots of calls throughout the day, take the same approach as with emails. Let them all build up and batch process at certain times throughout the day. Make sure you have a message bank to record the incoming messages. You might even leave a recorded message to explain to callers when you will check your calls throughout the day and set an expectation as to when they will hear from you.

When you are engaged in deep work, let all calls go to voicemail. During one of your multitasking breaks, you can check your phone, and snack, and check voicemail, all at the same time.

15-minute daily activity

Start by turning off all notifications from the apps on your phone and computer.

Lock in some times on your daily calendar to check email, schedule meetings and return phone calls.

Spend a few days working to your new schedule and when you are comfortable with how you are going, have some discussions with your boss, clients, coworkers, family members and housemates about scheduling times for regular activities. Make sure you hold them to the agreed schedule.

Stick up a reminder on the fridge or office door, so that people know when they can bother you and when to leave you alone. You might also want to set up an autoresponder on your emails, or a message on your phone which sets the expectation around when people will hear back from you.

If you work in an open-plan office, invest in some visibly large headphones and wear them during your "do not disturb" times.

Explore Coffee Shops

*"I have a group of coffee shops that I go to regularly ...
where I can do a couple of hours writing"—Bong Joon-ho*

Working and thinking are not the same things

No matter where you work, whether at home by yourself, home with a family, or at a separate workplace, there will always be distractions. It might be people; it might be laundry, or most likely, the fridge.

Add to this the fact that no matter how productive you are, not every type of activity thrives in the same location.

Clear thinking, for example, needs a different environment than other types of work. Writing might need a different location than checking emails. If you are lucky enough to work at a cool tech company, they will most likely provide pods, breakout rooms, or other dedicated thinking spaces. The rest of us aren't usually so lucky.

The trick is to find your own dedicated thinking space.

Coffee shops are a perfect third place

It might surprise you, but for most people, coffee shops are great thinking spaces. There is something about the noise and general busyness that provides a calming backdrop. It allows you to drift into your mind for a while. If you are one of those people who find any noise distracting, make sure you take a set of noise-cancelling headphones with you.

The great thing about coffee shops is the lack of any familiar distractions, such as the fridge or television. Once you order your drink and sit down, there is nothing else to do but grab your pen and notebook and start writing.

If you don't drink coffee or tea, there are plenty of other things you can order in a coffee shop which entitles you to 20-minutes of uninterrupted time.

I find my most productive days are when I visit three coffee shops in a row. I find the packing up and moving from one to another gives me some time to synthesise the ideas I just wrote down in the previous coffee shop. The best option is to visit a shopping centre with multiple options, walking distance from each other.

I find any shop where people know you; they are more likely to chat or come over and ask what you are doing. This is a disaster and will take you out of your focus zone. Find coffee shops where you are anonymous and will be left alone—bonus points for finding multiple coffee shops in the one location.

If one coffee shop is too busy, you can always move to another. It pays to find one empty enough to have your own space. Physically and mentally. Wearing visible headphones is a great way to shut out the noise and make it clear that you are not here to chat.

15-minute daily activity

Head out to a coffee shop with your pen and notebook in hand.

Once you place your order, sit away from other people and write in your journal. You can use continuous stream-of-consciousness writing or be deliberately creative in your journal.

There might be a particular project you are working on or a problem that needs solving. You might not have anything specific to think about, and you are hoping for some creative ideas to show up. Either way, a coffee shop will do the job.

Resist the urge to look at your phone. Stay with your notebook and allow your mind to wander on the page. There is something magical about a coffee shop for ushering your brain into the thinking/ writing zone.

Spend between 20-minutes to an hour in there and allow yourself time to think. Proper thinking time means you almost need to get bored. Don't distract yourself with the Internet. Allow your ideas to wander in of their own accord.

Clear Digital Clutter

"Clutter is not just the stuff on your floor. It is anything that stands between you and the life you want to be living"—Peter Walsh

Digital clutter is just as bad as physical clutter

There is a common variation of a meme that does the rounds of Facebook now and then, and it shows digital file names as final.psd, final final.psd, final final final.psd. Unless you have severe digital OCD, it is fair to say that the digital files on your phone or computer can quickly get out of hand.

I work at a university and get to peer over the shoulders of many staff and students. Nine times out of ten, I am greeted with a cluttered desktop. There is something about saving files when you are in the workflow process, especially when you are working on your computer, that makes it just easier to save it to the desktop and sort it out later.

At times, when work is chaos, I am just guilty as the next person of downloading a bunch of files to my downloads folder and rarely sorting through it.

There is research that suggests in a lifetime; we typically spend 5000 hours looking for things. I am better than most because I am in the habit of using a search facility rather than my memory. But every day I'll sit with people in front of the computer, and watch them search for files as they try to remember what they called them. This occupies way too much brainpower and time wasted looking for things.

One of the worst offenders for digital clutter for working professionals is the dreaded email. Emails are a terrible way to receive a variety of different types of information. Some people at my university have the awful habit of hitting "reply all" and sharing a group discussion in a string of emails. What is worse is somebody will attach something relevant to one of those nested email strings. If you are in the habit of skimming your emails multiple times a day, when it comes time to deal with things, you'll find yourself wasting time, trying to remember where you read it or finding who sent the attachment.

If you can make space in your email, and space on your computer, you will free-up space in your brain, your calendar, and your life.

Sort and systemise your digital life

There are two ways to deal with digital clutter: one is to sort, and one is to systemise.

Let's start with sorting. Chances are your emails are filled with junk, and files clutter your desktop. Recognising that it is impossible to stay tidy when you are working, it pays to set weekly or monthly reminders to have a digital clearout session.

A Friday afternoon tidy-up session can start in your office or workplace, and continue to your digital files. My Friday afternoon cleanups involve deleting everything in my downloads folder, if I don't need it, or moving it to a relevant folder in Dropbox if I do need it. I also apply the same process to my desktop files.

My email cleanup has to happen more often because I can receive hundreds of emails in one day. My goal at the end of the day is always to get to inbox zero.

Once you have cleared out your desktop, downloads folder, and email inbox, it is time to develop systems so that you don't get overwhelmed again.

Because I have multiple computers and work in various locations, I have to store everything in one place. I use an online storage service called Dropbox, though there are any number of online cloud storage services you could choose. I highly recommend using one of them to keep all your files stored in one place.

I used to carry my laptop around with me everywhere in case I needed a document which was on my computer. I would also spend many hours playing the hard-drive-shuffle trying to find where I had stored an old file, and I was forever trying to update my laptop to have the latest of everything.

It is not an exaggeration to say that moving everything to Dropbox has changed my life. It doesn't matter which device I have on me at the time; I can access all of my files from anywhere. I no longer have to remember which was the latest version; I no longer have to carry around hard drives or laptops. I no longer panic if my computer dies, because I know that all my files are stored safely in the cloud.

I have multiple email accounts, and so logging in and checking all of them is tedious. I switched to an email program called Polymail, which means all of my multiple email addresses are accessed through one application. Again, Polymail is a cloud storage service which means I can access it from any of my computers, plus my phone, or iPad. This helps me stay efficient because if I am trapped in long meetings all day, I can still be triaging my emails on my phone.

The mnemonic RADAR represents the system I have developed for dealing with my emails. Reduce, Archive, Delete, Action, Reply.

R is for Reduce
Start the system by reducing the number of emails you receive in the first place. Unsubscribe from all the emails you are no longer reading and try to be more explicit in the emails you send to reduce the number you will receive. For example, if you are arranging to meet someone, give them as much information as possible in the first email to reduce subsequent email ping pong.

A is for Archive

The next step in the system is to archive an email after you send it automatically. Polymail has this as a standard feature. Use it. Archive any emails you receive and might need again. Use the search feature to find it instead of having it sit in your inbox. You can also make folders to group archived emails.

D is for Delete

Delete any emails that you have read and won't need again later. Often people reply "thanks" or send through an FYI. Read it and delete it—no need to respond.

A is for Action

Once you have archived and deleted, you are left with all the emails which are asking you to do something. Look at each email and decide what you need to do with it. If it will take longer than two-minutes to action, add it to your to-do list as an action item and then move on to the next email.

R is for Reply

If you can reply to an email easily and in under two minutes, hit reply and deal with it then and there. Once you hit send, it should automatically archive (see A above), and then you can move on to the next email.

Get into the habit of using the RADAR system twice daily, and you will never feel overwhelmed by emails again.

15-minute daily activity

Sort through your computers, hard drives and email. Archive or Delete everything you can, and make a to-do list item to deal with everything you can't.

Start planning your digital system. Do you have multiple devices or email addresses? Start using Dropbox and Polymail to centralise everything.

Look at your daily workflow. Where are you getting overwhelmed? What system can you develop to deal with things as they come in?

Practice the RADAR system twice daily with your emails if inbox zero is currently something you only dream of.

Set up Your Portable Studio

"I can work anywhere"—Ray Bradbury

Feeling trapped can stifle creativity

For the majority of people living in a shared household, or with children and family, it can be tough to get some quiet thinking and working time. We all had to struggle with this during coronavirus lockdown.

Even if you live alone, or have a beautiful studio, there are still occasions where you might want to get away from it.

The creative mind needs stimulus, and also time to synthesise and process information. If you are chained to the same desk for eight hours a day or surrounded by chaos, it is challenging to think productively or concentrate for the full eight hours.

Repetitive tasks also wear down your energy levels and any ability to be creative, which is why getting up and moving around is so essential.

Unfortunately, people tend to expect the same work rate at 4 o'clock as you can produce at 9 o'clock. The fact is, we are not robots. Creative energy comes in waves throughout the day or week, and changes from person to person, depending on your cycle.

Expecting yourself to be able to produce eight hours of reliable output while sitting at the same desk is setting yourself up for failure.

Get up and move around

It is essential to work with your energy levels and also to experiment with movement. I don't mean exercise here, though of course getting up and going for a walk is a great way to refresh and restart your creative mind.

What I am talking about here is having different locations for different activities. For example, when I am in my studio and seated at the computer desk, the only tasks I do here is editing digital files and responding to emails.

If I need to write something, I move outside to the deck where I have a chair set up expressly for this purpose. I am currently sitting in my writing chair right now.

If I need to read something, I find this chair too uncomfortable, and I usually move myself to the couch for in-depth reading. When it is time to watch online courses or doodle on my iPad, I moved to the island bar in the kitchen.

I also have a similar pattern when I am at work. When I am in my office, I am either responding to emails or having meetings with people. If I need to write anything, I will get up and go for a walk to the nearest coffee shop. If I need to read or research anything, I will head up to the library.

After a while, if you regularly break your day by moving around to different locations, your subconscious will begin to associate the place with the type of task. This makes flicking the switch a lot easier than if you sit in the same chair for eight hours and expect your creative mind to be able to switch between different types of tasks.

I also use the act of moving from one location to another as a way to synthesise the information that I have just processed. Often, when I sit down in the next area, a burst of new ideas or a solution to the problem I was wrestling with will present itself.

This is how the subconscious works. Give it a problem to work on, and then stop thinking about it as you move from one location to another.

To be portable, you need to have a little tool kit that you can carry with you from place to place. My work colleagues are very used to seeing me walking along the corridor, clutching an iPad and a notebook in my hand.

If you need a laptop, invest in a carry bag or backpack so that you can take it with you to coffee shops or libraries.

Remember to be ready at all times to get to work, to capitalise on those moments where you are left waiting for somebody for 20 minutes. If someone is running late, rather than let it derail your day, always make sure you have a notebook or an iPad with you, or at the very least, a phone for taking notes.

For example, I am dictating the words you are currently reading on my iPhone rather than typing them. I am using an application called Dropbox Paper which automatically syncs with my computer. This means that I can keep writing anywhere, even if I don't have a notebook or an iPad.

I know that I always have my phone on me wherever I go, so I have set it up in a way that I can be as productive as possible, no matter where I am.

If you can afford it, an iPad or laptop is a crucial part of any portable studio. If your creative practice is more analogue, such as drawing or painting, it is still possible to make a portable little tool kit so that you can draw or paint no matter where you are.

My grandfather had an A5 block of watercolour paper, a jar of water with a screwtop lid, and a little Winsor and Newton metal watercolour kit that folded up nicely and even had a mixing palette on one side. He also had a watercolour brush with a cut-down handle which fit inside the metal kit. My grandfather celebrated every trip to the seaside with a tiny watercolour painting of boats—his favourite thing to paint.

The majority of craft activities can be just as portable. I love seeing people whip out knitting from their handbag at the bus stop. I also had a work colleague who would draw in a little pocket sketchbook during every boring work meeting he attended. By the time he retired, he had thousands of drawings of all of us in those pocket notebooks.

15-minute daily activity

List the things you will need for your portable studio.

Write down any issues you think you might struggle with making things portable, such as how to carry liquids or protect fragile items, if you are a painter or making physical objects.

Depending on your creative practice, and your specific set of issues, search for solutions once you know what your problems might be. On Pinterest, there are many terrific ideas for portable craft setups— foldable things, things on wheels, and bags with many pockets, to name a few.

Design a plan for your portable studio, and start collecting all of the things you will need.

Once your portable studio is equipped, keep it fully stocked and ready to grab whenever you leave the house.

Creative Retreats and Sabbaticals

"Sometimes you just need a break in a beautiful place. Alone. To figure everything out"—Unknown

Sometimes burnout is unavoidable

The majority of people in the full-time workforce have been sold on the promise that a lifetime of work will be rewarded with retirement. Halcyon days filled with travel and time to do all those things you dreamed of.

The problem is, for many, they have to continue working well beyond retirement age. For others, health and circumstance make enjoying retirement difficult, and for the majority, a lifetime of working trains us to be responsible and hardworking, rather than creative and playful.

On a smaller scale, the eight-hour day, five-day workweek pushes into the margins and sees people working longer hours or multiple jobs. Our pedal-to-the-metal lifestyle means that burnout is common, and we are never fully refreshed or restored by the weekends.

There is also a growing trend that the workforce doesn't take their annual leave. The pressure of returning to work after you have left it for three weeks unravels any benefit of the vacation, even if you could manage to take one.

Creative retreats can restore creativity

There are three types of creative sabbatical you might want to consider. The first one is easy. A weekly artist date. The second one takes some planning, a quarterly retreat. The third one takes a lot of planning, but it isn't impossible—a seventh-year sabbatical.

The purpose of all three is to rest, renew, refresh, and restore. For the quarterly or yearlong sabbatical, there is also the opportunity to complete a large project or create a masterwork.

Artist-in-residence programs serve this purpose very well. University lecturers often take a research sabbatical to finish a book or complete a significant research project.

Before you reject these ideas as entirely impossible, given your current circumstance, let's look at each one in more detail to see how they might be useful to consider.

Weekly

A weekly Artist Date was proposed as a concept by Julia Cameron in her book *The Artist's Way*.

The rules are simple. You must schedule and plan your weekly date with your inner artist as carefully as you would a date with another person, and you must go on each date alone.

Nothing is too frivolous. It doesn't have to be a trip to a gallery; a craft store is just as valid. It must be something which fills your creative well and restores your energy. You are giving some quality time and attention to your inner artist.

It is also a good idea to plan a different artist date every week. After you have exhausted all the predictable places, such as galleries and coffee shops, you will find yourself visiting all sorts of exciting places to renew your creativity, such as a second-hand record store or a toy shop.

Where will you take your inner artist this week?

Quarterly

While weekly Artist Dates are a lovely way to spend Saturday afternoon, you will no doubt be hijacked by household chores, social commitments, and all manner of life activity which will occupy the rest of your weekend. We all need uninterrupted time to think and create and write, which is where a creative retreat comes in.

Consider a weekend away every three months. A Creative Retreat gives you quality time to restore and refresh your energy but also to get some serious thinking and alone time. Schedule and book into a hotel or coworking space for a day or weekend every quarter.

Let your partner know what you are doing, if you have one, and if there are kids or pets to look after, schedule a sitter or trade your partner for a weekend where they can also get away every three months.

Creative Retreats take some planning and might feel decadent or self-indulgent, but if you have a creative project that just isn't getting done using any other method, this might be your best option.

What would it take to clear a day or a weekend, four times a year, and dedicate it to your creativity?

Sabbaticals

Focusing on retirement at the end of our working life is a mistake. Consider spreading your retirement throughout your working life instead.

Designer Stefan Sagmeister has built a yearlong sabbatical into his business model. He claims all the ideas he generates during his sabbatical year fuel his innovative and award-winning ideas when he returns to work. Every seven years he notifies all his clients and shuts up shop. By leaving Manhattan and heading to Bali for the year, he also dramatically reduces his living costs.

A laptop is all that is needed to run many online businesses, and so the desire to sell everything and hit the road for a year doesn't seem so impossible if you can continue to make money. Many bloggers sell everything and travel for a year, making money as they go.

Again, it might sound impossible from your current standpoint, but if you had to, what would it take to make it happen? Would you leave your job or take a hiatus? Could you sell your belongings or put them in storage? Could you rent out your house for a year?

Would you want to take the sabbatical at home? Could you plan long-service leave or go on reduced hours for reduced pay?

There are many ways to put the brakes on your current pace and give yourself a creative sabbatical. All it takes is a vision and some planning.

15-minute daily activity

Let's start planning your three different types of creative retreat.

Artist Dates

Brainstorm a list of free, or low-cost activities, which sound fun and silly, and you could do by yourself. They shouldn't be things you already do, like walking or going or the gym. Think galleries, quirky bookshops, craft stores, unusual exhibitions, music shops, and so on.

Schedule a morning or afternoon every week for the next six weeks: plan six fun and frivolous places to visit or activities to do. Lock them in your calendar and don't let anything get in the way.

Creative Retreats

Talk to your partner about what it would take for you to have a day or weekend away on your own. Help them understand it is to restore your creativity or finish a project, and that you are happy to trade them for a weekend where they can do the same thing.

If you are a free agent, book a weekend in a hotel or Airbnb. If you haven't got the funds available right now, find a place you like and start saving. If one night in a hotel three months from now is $120, you need to save $10 a week.

Creative Sabbatical

This is a free-thinking, brainstorming exercise. Write a list of things that would need to happen if, in seven years, you took a full year off.

How much money would you need? Where would you go?
What would you do? What would need to happen in year 1, 2, 3 and so on. to prepare for your year off? Write it down and pin it where you can see it.

If the idea excites you, start planning your sabbatical for real.

Conclusion

Creative Space was designed as a practical guide for busy people who want more space for creativity in their lives. This means that each of the 21 bite-sized activities are designed to be practical, actionable, and most importantly, quick.

In my experience, once you have cleared more headspace, you are able to concentrate on freeing up your calendar, and then you can move on to clearing a studio space and dedicate meaningful time and energy to your most important work. The effects of each of the activities in the book are cumulative.

While the book is short and you have probably read through it all in one sitting, I encourage you now to commit 15-minutes each day over the next three weeks and put each exercise into practice. Are you ready to commit to the 21-day Creative Space Challenge?

Epilogue

Ready to take the 21-day Creative Space Challenge?

Congratulations on making it to the end of the book. I hope you were able to get some value from the ideas contained within. To help you take the information and apply it to your circumstances, I have created a free companion course to help you get the most out of the 21 activities.

The free course includes downloadable worksheets, videos, and bonus resources. The materials are organised to match the sections and chapters of this book, making it easy for you to watch each video as you read along and complete the activities.

By the time you finish the Creative Space Challenge, you will have implemented the 21 strategies for living a more spacious and creative life.

Don't forget to visit the link to access to your free Creative Space bonus course now: creativespace.link/course

Afterword

So, where to from here?

I have created a podcast to help busy creatives just like you where I teach people how to clear space for creativity, discover your unique creative superpower and build a creative side-business. All of the podcast episodes are available for free, so if you would like to check it out, visit **www.creativesparkpodcast.com.**

Thank you for reading the book, and I would love to hear from you. Head over to Instagram and let me know what you thought of the Creative Space book and course.

You can find me at **@dominique_falla** and **@creativesparkpodcast**

About the Author

Dominique Falla is an author, artist, public speaker, and host of the Creative Spark Podcast. She helps busy creatives build thriving online businesses, and her mission is to help you keep your creative spark alive.